CONTENTS

S0-AZD-795

"The area of Salzburg, Naples, and Constantinople I hold to be the most beautiful in the world" wrote the world-travelling Alexander v. Humbold to a friend. He was certainly right. Salzburg's attraction is a mixture of the flair of the „Altstadt" (Old Town), the many magnificent churches and the old burghers' residences with their splendid facades. It is also the grandeur of the buildings of the prince-archbishops, the outstanding fortress, and the ever-present Wolfgang Amadeus Mozart, Salzburg's favourite son.

The countryside into which Salzburg is embedded furthers its appeal. The two wooded "city" mountains divided by the blue band of the flowing river Salzach provide splendid vantage

points to the city. In the north and east, Salzburg is surrounded by the Trumer Seenplatte and the Salzkammergut. There are abundant lakes for swimming and famous holiday locations. In the south and in the west, the foothills of the eastern Alps, often with snow covered summits make a resplendent backdrop for the city. A gentle, in-tuned mixture of culture, architecture, music, and nature - this is what makes Salzburg so attractive.

To really get to know Salzburg, you should take time. Walk over the Mönchsberg or the Kapzinerberg and see the city from all sides. Stroll comfortably through the little alleys, slowly take in the splendour of the magnificent buildings or visit some of the many museums.

Historical Overview

Salt mining has an early history at Dürrnberg above Hallein. Salt was mined then shipped down the river Salzach.

The first settlements date back to the Stone Age. The heyday of the salt mining was from 800-400 BC during the time of the Celts.

ca. 100 BC
The Celtic principality Noricum comes into being from parts of what are today the provinces of Salzburg, Tyrol, Carinthia and Upper Austria.

It is economically and culturally highly developed and enjoys trade relations with the Holy Roman Empire.

14 BC
The Romans conquer the Celtic principality and establish the settlement „Juvavum" around the area of what is today Salzburg's „Old Town".

ca. 45 AD
Juvavum receives its town charter from Emperor Claudius and experiences a time of prosperity.

170 - 180
During the Marcomannian Wars the city is destroyed.

ca. 210
The Roman Emperor Severius restores order and the rebuilding begins.

ca. 470
Saint Severin works in Noricum.

ca. 500
The city falls into ruin during the turmoil of a period of a mass migration after invasions of German tribes.

696

The Franconian Bishop Rupert founds on the ruins of Juvavum the monastery of St.Peter and the convent Nonnberg. Following this, is the city at times the seat of the Bavarian Dukes.

739

Saint Boniface founds the Bavarian dioceses, which includes Salzburg. The abbot of St.Peter's is appointed as bishop.

746 - 784

St.Virgil is bishop. He has a cathedral with three naves built and supports art and culture.

755

The name Salzburg first appears in a document on the life of the St.Boniface.

798

Salzburg is elevated to an arch-bishopric and is given rich land-holdings and salt mining rights on Dürrnberg.

987

Archbishop Friedrich I divides St.Peter's Abbey from the archbishopric. The Cathedral Chapter now elects the bishops who are also secular princes.

Romanesque fresko, Nonnberg

996

Emperor Otto III grants Salzburg market, toll and coinage rights.

1077

Archbishop Gebhard establishes the Hohensalzburg Fortress.

1167

Emperor Barbarossa put Salzburg under the ban of the Empire and lets it be burned to the ground.

1181

Archbishop Konrad III pushes forward reconstruction of the city and the construction of the large Romanesque cathedral, (much larger than it is today).

5

ArchbishopWolf Dietrich
Kaspar Memberger (1589)
Salzburg Museum

1200
The first bridge is built over the Salzach River.

1328
ArchbishopFriedrichv.Leibnitz enacts the first Salzburg Provincial Order and with that carries out the conclusive separation from Bavaria.

1348
The plague rages through the city and one -third of the population dies.

1368
Documentary evidence of the city charter under Archbishop Pilgrim can be found.

1481
Salzburg receives the rights of an imperial city under Emperor Friedrich III.

1495 - 1519
Archbishop Leonhard v. Keutschach has the fortress further expanded to the size it is today.

1525
A peasant uprising against Church authority. The Fortress, in which the hated archbishop is hidden, is besieged for three months without success.

1541
The doctor Paracelsus works for a short time in the city. He dies here.

1587 - 1612
The features of the city are fundamentally altered under Archbishop Wolf Dietrich von Raitenau. Through the demolition of a complete city quarter and the creation of spacious plazas he turns Salzburg into a royal seat. The Residenz, the present day's Baroque cathedral, Mirabell Castle and the Capuchin Monastery come into being. He resigns after a conflict with Bavaria and is held prisoner until his death.

1612 - 1619
The pleasure castle Hellbrunn is constructed under Archbishop Markus Sittikus v. Hohenems.

1619 - 1653
Archbishop Paris Lodron made the city defence-ready through extensive fortifications.

1623
The first university is founded.

1628
The cathedral is completed.

1687 - 1709
Archbishop Johann Ernst Graf v. Thun assigns the famous master builder Fischer v. Erlach as the architect of his court. Important buildings such as the Dreifaltigkeitskirche (Holy Trinity Church), Ursuline Church, and the Klessheim Castle are built.

1727 - 1744
Under the rule of Archbishop Leopold v. Firmian, 22.000 Protestants are expelled from the country. He also built Leopoldskron Castle.

1756
Wolfgang Amadeus Mozart is born on January 27 in Nr. 9 Getreidegasse.

1772 - 1803
The unsuccessful and unpopular Archbishop Hieronimus Colloredo flees in 1800 from French troops under Napoleon and in 1803 while in exile in Vienna renounces his princely claims. This ends the period of Church rule in Salzburg.

The Grand Duke of Tuscany Ferdinand von Habsburg-Lothringen takes over the principality and has the

Archbishop Markus Sittikus

7

Wolfgang Amadeus Mozart

treasures of the church brought to Italy.

1806 - 1809
Salzburg is a part of Austria for the first time.

1810 - 1815
The occupation through Bavaria means the loss of the last remaining art treasures.

1816
Salzburg finally comes to Austria.

1818
A large part of the New Town is destroyed by a violent fire.

In the Nikolaus Chapel in Oberndorf near Salzburg, the Christmas carol "Silent Night" is heard for the first time.

1860 - 1866
The old city walls are torn down, the Salzach regulated, and the city is expanded.

1920
The Salzburg Festival is established by Max Reinhardt and Hugo v. Hoffmannsthal. "Jedermann" is performed for the first time on the plaza in front of the Cathedral.

1926
The Salzburg airport is opened.

1938
The invasion of German troops in Austria. Salzburg becomes a Reich's District.

1944/45
The city's cultural monuments are heavily damaged by allied air raids.

1944 - 55
Salzburg is occupied by American troops.

1960
Marks the festive opening of the new Large Festival Theatre.

1962
Salzburg University is re-established.

1966
The establishment of the Salzburg Easter Festival under the direction of Herbert v. Karajan.

1989
Herbert von Karajan dies. He is buried in Anif near Salzburg.

1991
The province of Salzburg celebrates the 200th anniversary of the death of Mozart with a large exhibition in Klessheim Castle.

1994 - 96
The home of the Mozart family is restored to its original form.

Through the „Altstadt" (Old Town)

Residenzplatz - Dom - Festung - Stift Nonnberg - Mozartplatz - Alter Markt - Getreidegasse - Mönchsberg - Museumsplatz - Pferdeschwemme - Festspielhaus - St.Peter - Franziskanerkirche - Universitätsplatz

(1) We begin our city tour at the ***Residenzplatz***, the largest square in the Old Town. It lies between the residence of the former prince-archbishops and the Residenz-Neugebäude (New Building). It is bordered on the north by the former burgher's city and on the south by the cathedral. At the time of the Romanesque cathedral, the area was a cemetery. In the middle of the square, rises the 15 m. ***Residenzbrunnen (Residence Fountain).*** It was created by Italian sculptor Tommaso di

Garona between (1656-61) and is said to be the largest and most beautiful Baroque fountain outside of Italy. Four water-spouting horses surround a large rock on which stand three giants supporting a large dish on their shoulders. Inside are large fish holding another dish with their tails. The king of the sea, Triton sits here and blows a water stream through a conch into the air.

The *New Residence* on the east side of the Residenzplatz houses the Salzburg-Museum, which presents an exiting insight into Salzburg's history, art and culture *(☞ page 108)*. Archbishop Wolf Dietrich had the palace built in 1592 - 1602 to house his guests. The state rooms on the second floor *(Ständesaal, Bishop's Hall, Portrait Room)* are decorated with colourful stucco-work of exceptional beauty.

The building was later enlarged by Archbishop Kuenburg. In 1702 Achbishop Thun added the characteristic **belltower.** The 35 bells of the carillon still chime daily at 7 and 11am and at 6pm. with melodies by Mozart, Schubert and Haydn.

On the other side of the square stands the *"Old Residence"*. It was the seat of the Salzburg prince-archbishops from the 12th century to 1803. Today's Renaissance building was begun in 1595 under Archbishop Wolf Dietrich and further enlarged by his successors. From the 180 rooms of the Residenz, it is the staterooms, above all, that reflect the worldly power and wealth of the prince-bishops. Today they can be viewed and offer a beautiful space for evening concerts and receptions.
(☞ *Residence, page 108*)

One enters the Residenz through a splendid portal of Untersberg marble (1610). In the back left corner of the interior court-yard (next to the Hercules Fountain) a long stairway with low, flat steps leads up to the staterooms on the second story. The wonderful stucco-work on the walls and ceiling stem from

Conference Room

Alberto Camesina, the splendid ceiling fresco from Johann Michael Rottmayr and Martino Altomonte.

The tour begins in the *Carabinieri Hall,* the largest hall measuring 50 m long, 12 m wide and 12 m high. It served as the entertainment and practice hall for the princely bodyguards. The large ceiling fresco from Rottmayr impressively shows the „Four Elements". In the *Knight's Hall* chamber-concerts are held today just as they once were. The marvellous ceiling frescoes depict the life of Alexander the Great.

We move further to the *Conference Room* where in addition to conferences, concerts were held. It is here that six-year-old Mozart held his first concert. In the *Antecamera* (the Antechamber) you'll see next to the lovely tapestries, a beautiful stove with a gilded vase. The *Audience Room* was

14

furnished with valuable Gobelin tapestries and furniture. The stucco is covered with gold leaf. We continue with the princely Work Room, the writing and casket rooms, where documents and money were kept. Then on to the Bedroom and to the „Beautiful Gallery"

Ceiling-painting in the „Beautiful galerie"

where the princely paintings are displayed. The *Throne Room* with valuable silk tapestries on the walls, the *White Hall*, the *Green Room* and the *Emperor Hall*, with paintings of the Habsburg emperors and kings brings the tour to an end.

The **Residence Gallery** on the third floor houses an important collection of paintings from the 16th to the 19th century, including paintings from Rembrandt, Rubens, Titian, Lesueur, and others (☞ *page 108*).

In front of the Residence is the stand of the horse-drawn hackney cabs called **"Fiaker".** From here, You can start Your tour of the city by carriage.

Waldmüller, "Children at the window"

15

Through the Cathedral arches you reach the **Domplatz** *(Cathedral Square)* with the **Mariensäule** *(„Virgin's Column")* built by Hagenauer brothers in 1771. They symbolise the triumph of the Church over the power of evil. The figures on the base personify wisdom, the Church, the angels, and the Devil.

Under the archway is the entrance the subterranean **Excavations Museum** where the remains of the old cathedral foundations can be viewed *(☞ page 108)*.

Every year during the summer Salzburg Festival, Hugo v. Hoffmannsthal's **"*Jedermann*"** *("Everyman")* is presented the story of the life and death of a rich man, with the splendid jointed Baroque facades of the Cathedral as a backdrop.

The majestic **Cathedral** is the most significant Italian monumental structure north of the Alps and already the third church construction in the same location. The first cathedral was built in 767-774 under Abbot and Bishop Virgil. In the 12th century Virgil's Cathedral was replaced with a Romanesque basilica with five naves and five spires. A fire damaged the Romaneque cathedral so badly in 1598 that Archbishop Wolf Dietrich decided on a new building and had the old one torn down.

Gate of Hope

The construction of today's cathedral, following the plans of the Italian court architect Santino Solari, began in 1614 under Archbishop Markus Sittikus. The house of God was consecrated by Archbishop Paris Lodron in 1628; the towers however were not completed until 1655.

Untersberg marble was used for the three-story façade and four-story spires. In front of the arched -shaped entrance portals one can see the statues of patron saints Rupert and Virgil (outside) as well as those of the apostles Peter and Paul (inside). Halfway up the façade are the four evangelists and on the gable, left and right the prophets Moses and Elijah and Christ stands on the top. One enters the Cathedral through three heavy bronze portals with the symbols faith, love and hope that were built in 1958.

The interior of the Cathedral (length 86 m. width 62,5 m.) is in a cool white and holds over 10.000 people. The ceiling frescoes in the middle nave were painted by Arsenio Mascagni and Ignazio Solari and show scenes of the life and suffering of Christ and lead to Mascagni's large picture of the resurrection of Christ.

The frescoes of the 71 m high octagonal cupola show occurrences out of the Old Testament. In 1944, the cupola was badly damaged by allied bombs. The rebuilding and the reconstruction of the frescoes were finished in 1959.

The new organ in the old Baroque housing.

Beneath the crossing of the nave and transept, one finds the crypts built in 1959 on the remains of the earlier cathedral. They are the burial place of the Salzburg Archbishops. A Romanesque crucifix of the 13th century can be found in the crypt chapel.

The **baptismal font** resting on bronze lions located in the first chapel on the left also stems out

of Romanesque cathedral and was cast in 1321. The cover was newly designed in 1959.

The **Cathedral Museum** *(entrance in the narthex, right)* houses valuable pieces of old Cathedral Treasure and a reconstruction of the "Art and Rarity Chamber" of the Salzburg Archbishops.

(☞ Cathedral Museum, page 108)

On the south side of the Cathedral is the large **Kapitelplatz**. Behind on the left is the **Neptune's Fountain** *(Neptunbrunnen)*. It was built in 1732 by the sculptor Anton Pfaffinger and was one of the horse ponds of the Cathedral Chapter. The Pegasus statue that once stood here now stands in Mirabell Gardens.

In the south-east corner of the square is a side entrance to St.Peter's Cemetery. Following straight-ahead one will reach the Fortress.

The **Hohensalzburg Fortress**, the symbol of the city, is the largest and the best-preserved citadel in Europe. The construction was begun in 1077 under Archbishop Gebhard. Up to the 17th century it was constantly being enlarged and fortified with towers, bastions, walls, and entrenchments. The fortress achieved its present day form under Archbishop Leonhard

von Keutschach in the 15th century. It was made livable, was richly furnished and was given its late Gothic appearance. One can see overall on the fortress walls its coat of arms, a turnip. On the exterior wall of the Fortress Chapel is a marble relief of the archbishop.

A funicular railway brings one comfortably up to Hasengrabenbastei (one of the bastions of the Fortress). An alternative is a 10-minute walk by way of the Festungsgasse.

(☞ Our tip: Take the funicular up and walk down passing through the defence-fortifications of the fortress. Stop for a break at the Stieglkeller Gastgarten situated above the Festungsgasse.)

1. Mayor's-Tower
2. Mesnerstöckl
3. Tower of the trumpet
4. Kuenburg-Bastion
5. St.George's Chapel
6. Hoher Stock
7. Bell-Tower
8. Reck-Tower
9. Hasengraben-Bastion
10. Keutschach-Archway

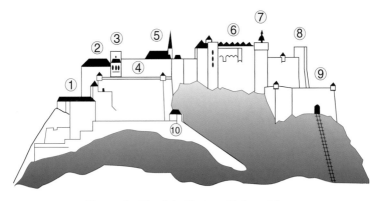

The north-side of the Fortress Hohensalzburg

The „**Golden Chamber**" is a part of the late Gothic State Apartments that were built on the fourth floor of the *"Hohen*

Stocks" (Inner Castle) in 1501 under Archbishop Leonhard. Viewing the royal chambers is possible only with guided tour. The walls and ceiling is panelled and rich with gilded and painted wooden ornamentation. The *majolica ceramic oven* also from 1501 is one of the most spectacular examples of stove-fitter's art of the time.

The blue ceiling of the *"Golden Hall"* is decorated with countless gold buttons, like twinkling stars in the night sky. Supporting the ceiling are four massive pillars with twisted stems, a frieze decorates the long ceiling joist.

Also during the tour one can see a part of the battlement walkway, the gruesome torture chamber and the *"Salzburger Stier" (Steer)*, an organ, the loud tones of which once were a reminder of the morning opening and evening closing of the city gates.

In the **Fortress Museum** one can find interesting weapons and pieces of equipment as well as everything over the history of the Hohensalzburg Fortress. (☞ *Fortress museum, page 108*)

A guided tour is not required to enjoy the picturesque courtyard, the large linden tree, the cistern and St.George's Chapel, as well as numerous scenic views.

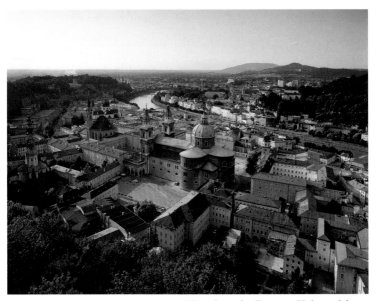

View from the Fortress Hohensalzburg

From the Fortress walls one has a marvellous view of the city, the surrounding mountains and the foothills of the Alps.

The fortress was once besieged but never captured. The story of the *"Salzburger Stierwascher"* *(Salzburg Steer-Wash)* is famous. During a long period of siege the last steer was painted daily with new paint and lead to the outer defence wall to graze and then back to be washed off. The attackers were so convinced of the large surplus of provisions that they gave up the siege disappointed.

Only the French troops under Napolean surrendered without a fight. They expressed their thanks in their own way and took all the weapons and equipment they could carry with them.

(8) If you keep to the right as you walk down from the fortress, you will come to the *Nonnberg Convent,* the oldest convent north of the Alps. St.Rupert founded it on the most eastern ridge of the Fortress Mountain in 700.

He installed his niece, Erentrudis, (later St.Erentrudis) as the first abbess. Noteworthy is the main doorway to the church (1499) in which a late Romanesque tympanum from 1210 was incorporated.

The Gothic church interior is formed with interesting reticulated rib vaulting, especially worth seeing is that on the 18 resting columns in the crypt under the choir. The high alter stems from the year 1515, the carved wooden alter in the lateral St.John's Chapel is from the year 1498 and is probably from sculptor Veit Stoß. Beneath the choir several murals were exposed from the middle of the 12th century.

From the Nonnberg Convent one can either come down the Nonnberg Steps into the Kaigasse or make a small detour through a part of the city called Nonntal on the eastern foot of the Fortress Mountain. (☞ *Follow the Nonnberggasse, branch off to the left and climb the steps to Nonntaler Hauptstraße.*)

St. Erhard Church originally belonged to the Nonnberg Convent and was the church of the small Convent Hospital. The unconventional façade is situated in front of the columned portal built during the new construction done under the architect Gasparo Zuccalli from 1685-89.

Through the narrow Schanzlgasse you will come to **Kajetanerplatz.** The large plain building on the right is the Justice Building. Following is the **Kajetanerkirche** *(St.Cajetan's Church)*, a Baroque construction without towers, but with a powerful oval dome. It was also built

by Architect Zucalli as a convent church for the Order of the Theatines, the founder of which was St.Cajetan. The dome fresco „*Glory to St.Cajetan*" as well as the high alter painting are from the artist Paul Troger.

29

Follow the Kaigasse and you reach **Mozartplatz.** It is
bordered on the west by the Residenzplatz and came into being
as a result of the tearing down of a number of housing groups
in 1588 during the time of Archbishop Wolf Dietrich. Around
the square, next to the Residenz-Neugebäude more splendid
residences were built including the Andretter-Haus
(No.4, with the attractive chapel in the inner courtyard)
or the Imhofstöckl (No.5, around 1620).

The bronze Wolfgang Amadeus Mozart statue was cere-
moniously unveiled in the presence of Mozart's two sons in
1842. *(☞ Our tip: Enjoy a cup of coffee at a nearby Café and
watch the hustle and bustle on the square.)*

31

The little **Michaelskirche** *(St.Michael's Church)* integrated into the row of houses on the Residenzplatz, was the oldest parish church in the city until 1139 and probably was built in 788. It was altered many times and received its late Baroque appearance in 1767-1776. The interior houses Rococo stucco-work (from Benedikt Zöpf, 1769) and interesting ceiling frescoes that are worth seeing.

The burghers' city begins north, behind St.Michael's Church, formed with its houses crowded together and its narrow lanes. This is in contrast to the well-planned and generously laid out Bishop's city. The **Waagplatz** was once the centre of the burgher city. The business people moved here; markets and legal handling were done. From 1328 Waagplatz No.1 was the first City Hall in Salzburg.

In house No.1a in 1887 the lyric poet **Georg Trakl** was born. The room in which he was born is now a memorial with autographs and other memorabilia *(☞ page 108)*.

Through the narrow **Judengasse** you'll reach **Alter Markt** *(Old Market)*. Notice the little side streets, *Brodgasse and Goldgasse*. Around 1300, in the course of city expansion the main market was moved here. The square is framed by the ornamented medieval burghers' houses. In the middle stands

the octagonal market fountain with its artistic scrollwork grill adorning a statue of St.Florian, the patron saint against the dreaded fire. The *Hofapotheke,* (Prince-

archbishop's Court Pharmacy, house no. 6), with its Rococo furnishing was founded in 1591 and is worth seeing. Opposite you'll see the city's „smallest house" and next to that is the Café Tomaselli, the oldest café in the city (1703).

(15) The ***City Hall*** on the Kranzlmarkt is a typical example of modesty of the Salzburg middle class. It is hard to find such a small plain building in another city of comparable size. In the year 1407 the City Council was moved here from Waagplatz. In 1772 the building was renovated, it received the Rococo façade and the figure of Justice (1617, from Hans Waldburger) over the entrance portal.

(16) ***Getreidegasse***, the sustained street of the medieval free city, counts today as the most important shopping street the Mozart city and is frequented by countless tourists. Its name has nothing to do with "Getreide" (grain); rather, it is related to „traben" (run).

This narrow street has became famous with the many gilt and wrought-iron signs identifying the guilds of craftsmen who once lived here and offered their products and services.

The houses, partly from the period of the 13-16th centuries mostly have charming interior courtyards and passageways decorated with columns and vaulted ceilings. The passageway lead into the Universitätsplatz Good examples are house no.3, no.7 and no.25.

(17) At No.9 Getreidegasse, on 27 January 1756, ***Wolfgang Amadeus Mozart,*** the famous composer was born. Mozart's father Leopold, was Archiepiscopal Court Music Director and had rented the apartment on the third floor. The house is now owned by the Mozarteum Foundation and today houses an exhibition of pictures and documents of the Mozart family as well as instruments that belonged to Mozart, for example, his harpsichord, the violin he played as a small child. Other rooms show an exhibit about Mozart and the theatre, as well as the middle class style of décor during Mozart's time (☞ *page 108*).

(18) At the end of Getreidegasse one comes to the **Blasiuskirche** *(Church of St.Blaise, 1350)*. It was built as the church for the Burgher Hospital which accounts for its simple outside appearance. A small chapel originally stood on this site, dedicated to St.Blaise. The Gothic interior is formed with characteristic reticulated ribbed vaulting over slim columns. In the 15th century an additional gallery was added for the sick.

(19) The **Bürgerspital** *(Burghers' Hospital)* came into being between 1556 and 1570 and was in dissolved in 1898. The building with its beautiful Renaissance arcaded courtyard houses today collections from the Salzburg-Museum, including a special collection of old toys

(☞ *page 108*). As we go through the **Gstättentor** turn right behind St.Blaise's Church and walk 50 m. to the Mönchsberglift. *(operating daily from 9am-11pm)*. Take the lift up and enjoy one of the most beautiful views of the city's Old Town.

(22) The **Museum der Moderne Salzburg-Mönchsberg** shows modern art of famous workers. (☞ *page 108*)

The 500 m high **Mönchsberg** encloses the Old Town to the southwest. The partially vertical rock walls must be regularly checked by the "Bergputzern" (mountain-cleaners), to remove loose rock and bushes and thus prevent landslides, (the last catastrophe in 1669 killed over 200 people.)

Numerous paths with many marvellous views of the Old Town lead from here over the Mönchsberg. Following on to the right one reaches the area of Mülln. Here you'll find the earthy **Augustiner Bräustübl** (Augustine Brewery Inn) where you should allow yourself a good litre tankard of beer and a hearty snack. On hot summer days hundreds of thirsty visitors relax in the shady Gastgarten.

If you go up the Mönchsberg to the left, you go by the *Stadtalm-Inn,* which also offers a terrace with a beautiful view of the Old Town. Here you can also see a part of the city's fortification, constructed under Archbishop Paris Lodron, in which the complete mountain was encircled. The path leads further to the fortress, a narrow stairway branches off to the left and down to the Festival House. Further departures lead into the Reichenhaller Straße on the backside of the Neutor or in the Nonntal district of the city *(through the "Bürgermeisterloch").*

One can also take the *Mönchsberg-lift* down and turn left to the *Museumplatz,* where you'll find another interesting museum:

The **Haus der Natur** *(one should plan to take a whole day)* displays on 4 floors, animals, plants, minerals, and unusual things from all over the world. In aquariums, you'll see local fresh water fish and colourful tropical fish, a terrarium with over 200 snakes, lizards, frogs and crocodiles. The Space Hall and the Dinosaur-Exhibit located on the ground level are also impressive. (☞ *page 108*)

Through the narrow Gstättengasse (the houses on the left are nestled tightly on the Mönchsberg) one reaches **Ursulinenplatz**. The **Markuskirche** or *Ursulinenkirche (St.Mark's or Ursuline Church)* was built for the Ursuline Order from a design by Fischer von Erlach in 1699-1705. This was the same site of the earlier hospital and church of the Order of the Brothers of Mercy. Both buildings were destroyed in a landslide in 1699.

Directly connected to the church is the section of the former Ursuline Convent since 1959 serving the House of Nature as an exhibition area. The interior of the Baroque church is adorned with stuccowork and vault frescos.

The **Klausentor** *(Klausen Gate)* was built on the narrow area between the Mönchberg and the Salzach and was earlier the outer city gate to the west.

41

A detour to **Mülln:** The district called Mülln with its narrow roads received its name from the original mills that were built here. **The Müllner Kirche** or *Marienkirche (St.Mary's Church)* visible over a long distance, was already being mentioned in documents as early as 1148. The Baroque style that it has today was created in 1673-1738. In the church interior you can see Baroque wagon vault, the late Gothic reticulated rib vault situated above was maintained.

(24)

The church is connected by an arch to the monastery building of the Augustinian Hermits. Since 1890 has been renown as a brewery inn called **Augustinerbräu or Müllnerbräu** (☞ *page 39*).

Across from the Müllnerbräu you'll see the large grounds of the Provincial Hospital. In the middle is the **St.Johannesspitalkirche** 1699-1704 *(St.John's Hospital Church)*, the fourth Baroque church in Salzburg built by Fischer von Erlach.

Along the Salzach River or over the Mönchsberg we come back to the Old Town of Salzburg again and continue our sightseeing round with the Festival District.

The ***Pferdeschwemme (Horse Pond)*** was built in 1695. The horses from the archbishop's stables were washed here. It was designed by Fischer v. Erlach and the horse frescos were made **(25)** by the Court painter Franz Anton Ebner. In the centre stands a statue of horse being trained. It was created by sculptor Michael Mandl. The splendid Horse Pond underlines the importance of horses in the Baroque period. Behind the Horse Pond you can see the ***Sigmundstor*** (also called the Neutor) completed in the 18th century. It connects the Old Town to a part of the city known as Riedenburg.

Now you come to the Hofstallgasse. In the house on the left the University Library and Assembly Hall are located. On the right side You find the *Festival Theatres* (the Large Festival Theatre, the „House of Mozart" and the Felsenreitschule).

(26)

The *Large Festival Theatre* was built (1956-1960) following the plans of the master builder Clemens v. Holzmeister on the site of the former Court stables. For decades the world famous

Large Festival Theatre

conductor Herbert v. Karajan worked here. The giant auditorium, well known for its good acoustics holds 2.500 people and was cut out of the rock of the Mönchsberg. The old court stables were rebuilt as an entrance foyer and inter-mission hall (☞ *page 108)*.

The new festival theatre **„House for Mozart"** was built in 2006. In the **Felsenreitschule**, with arcaded galleries hewn from the rock once held jousting tournaments and animal baiting. Today it is the venue for monumental operas and theatre works.

House for Mozart

Across from the Festival Theatres You will find *The Wild Mann Fountain* and behind it a small park, which was once the botanical garden of the University. The **Kollegienkirche** (☞ *page 51*) stands next to it. On the corner of Hofstallgasse and Franzikanergasse, you'll find the **Museum of Modern Art Salzburg-Rupertinum** (☞ *page 108*).

Turn to the right into the Toscaninihof, (the Toscanini Courtyard) and you'll find the entrance to the Altstadt Parking Garage and the stairs leading up to the Mönchsberg.

The way left leads through an archway into the **St.Peter's District** and the oldest existing abbey in the German speaking region founded by Bishop Rupert in 696. The first inner courtyard, the Kollege St.Benedikt, (St.Benedict's College) is the newest tract of the abbey. The theological seminary was built in 1924-26 replacing the old working quarters.

In the arched gateway to the next courtyard one can find a monument to **Michael Haydn.** Scores and personal items belonging to the composer, whose life and musical creations were closely connected to the seminary, are available to see (☞ *page 108*).

The picturesque second of the three inner courtyards is called the Outer Abbey Court. The hexagonal fountain in the middle was previously used for fish. The three-aisled **St. Peter's Abbey Church** was built in 1130-1143 replacing the burned Romanesque church. In the middle of the 17th and the 18th centuries it was made into a Baroque style, the façade was redesigned, the cupola and the onion shaped tower were added.

In the splendid Rococo interior one can still see in some details the Romanesque original (in the staired portal, for example). Sixteen graduated marble alters lead in hierarchical order to the high altar (from Lorenz Hörmbler), showing Peter, Paul and Benedict seeking intecession from the Mother of God. Notice the spendid organ over the entrance. The church also houses numerous monuments including that of St. Rupert.

To the right next to the church the idyllic **St. Peter's Cemetery** is located, the oldest Christian cemetery in Salzburg. Here you will find the graves of many well-known and prominent people, the composer Michael Haydn for example, and the cathedral architect Santino Solari.

In the middle of the cemetery is the Gothic **St.Margaret Chapel,** built in 1491, with the old memorial slabs on the outer wall. Over the archways, built in 1626, on the Mönchsberg side, you will see the **Katakomben** *(Catacombs)* where early

Christian prayer sites are hewn into the cliff *(☞ page 108).*

The entrance to the chapels in the cave can be found on the right behind the Chapel of the Holy Cross, in the first arcade at the rock. Steep steps lead upward to *St.Gertrude's Chapel.* Six curved niches divide the stone wall with partial frescoes depicting the martydom of Thomas Becket. Climbing up the stone steps further one reaches the *Maximus Chapel* with a copy of an early Christian martyr's grave in a

stone niche. On the east side of the cemetery to exits are to be found, one leads to the Festungsgasse (next to the valley station of the Fortress Railway, the other leads by the rushing *Almbach* on to the Kapitalplatz. The third Abbey courtyard of St.Peter, surrounds the oldest part of the monestary, is a part of the cloister enclosure and is not open to the public. Here are also found the remains of the old Romanesque cloister.

We leave the St.Peter's district, and come to the *Franziskanerkirche (Franciscan Church)*. It is connected to the cloister by a flying buttress. It was earlier a chapel of the St.Peter's Convent, and later was the parish church and convent church of the Nuns of St.Peter. During the great city fire (1167), the late Romanesque nave remained virtually undamaged. It was expanded in the 15th century with a towering Gothic chancel and a beautiful high altar by Michael Pacher. The appointment of the Franciscans in place of the Nuns of St.Peter was through Archbishop Wolf Dietrich and is how the church with its steep Gothic tower came to have its current name. The Baroque high altar is the work Fischer v. Erlach.

He rebuilt it in 1709 but incorporated the Gothic *Madonna by Michael Pacher.*

Through the Sigmund-Haffner-Gasse in the direction of the Rathaus we turn left through the Ritzerbogen onto the *Universitätsplatz.* Weekdays, dealers offer a variety of fruit, vegetables, cheese, and smoked meats at the open market.

The square is dominated by the splendid façade of the white *Kollegienkirche, (Collegiate Church),* the Baroque masterpiece of Fischer v. Erlach. Archbishop Thun commissioned the church for the University and it was constructed in 1696-1707. The long main aisle dominates the bright and high interior. The figures on the high altar are by Josef Pfaffinger.

(29)

A Walk in the New Town

Makartplatz - Mirabellgarten - Loreto-Kirche - Sebastian-Friedhof - Linzergasse - Kapuzinerberg

From the lower end of Hanusch Platz, you cross the Salzach over the Markart Footbridge to the ***Markartplatz.*** To the right you'll see ***Mozart Residence.*** The Mozart family lived there from 1773-1787 after the little apartment on Getreidegasse became too small. Bombing during World War II largely destroyed the residence. In 1994-96 it was renovated and returned to its original design with the help of a Japanese investor through the Mozarteum Foundation. The exhibit housed here is worth seeing. It shows the Mozart family and

the Salzburg of 1773-1787. The ***Tanzmeistersaal*** *(Dancing Master's Hall)* remains in its original state and is used for concerts.

The Markartplatz is dominated by the **Dreifaltigkeits- kirche** *(Holy Trinity Church)* 1694-1703 an early masterpiece of the architect Fischer v. Erlach. It is the monastery church of the Priesterhaus, which is situated on both sides of the church around two interior  courtyards. After the big city fire of 1818 the towers on this magnificent construction were reconstructed, increasing the

height and accentuating them, the Baroque character, however was maintained.

The interior of the church is adorned with among other things, extensive stuccowork, a noteworthy dome fresco by Johann Rottmayr (approx. 1700) and the very beautiful high altar also designed by Fischer v. Erlach.

Across from Mozart Residence, you will see the expansive Hotel Bristol, then the *Salzburger Landestheater (Salzburg Provincial Theatre)*. It was built in 1892-93 in place of the old Ballhaus and was renovated and enlarged in 1938. In between these two building you'll find the main entrance to Mirabell Gardens.

Take a quick look around the corner on Schwarzstraße. Here you'll find the Kammerspiele (Studio Theatre) of the Landestheater and the world famous *Marionettentheater (Marionette Theatre)* which has played its repertoire of Mozart operas to enthusiastic audiences the world over. Next comes the *Mozarteum*, Salzburg's music college. The Art Nouveau bulding houses next to the school-

tract numerous halls for orchestra, chamber and solo performances. In the garden is the *Zauberflöten-häuschen (The House of the Magic Flute)* in which Mozart is supposed to have composed his last opera.

The **Mirabellgarten** *(Mirabell Gardens)* displays to its visitors a colourful world of flowers and sculptures, artistically trimmed hedges and arbours, blossoms and water-spouting fountains. In 1606 Archbishop Wolf Dietrich built for his mistress Salome Alt the castle *"Altenau"* at the gates of the city. His successors enlarged it and made it the summer residence of the archbishops and called it Mirabell. The form of today's garden follows the 1690 plan designed by Fischer von Erlach.

We enter the *"Large Garden"* of the park through a gate with pedestals on which stand stone fencers. On the balustrades left and right are crowded the gods of antiquity.

55

Surrounding the high fountain in the middle you'll find four groups of figures by the sculptor Ottavio Mosto. They portray the elements air, earth, fire, and water through mythological association; Paris stealing Helena over water, Pluto abducting Persophone beneath the earth, Hercules lifting the giant Anteus into the air, and Aeneas rescuing his father Anchises from the burning Troy.

Right of the fountain in the former orangery you'll find the **Baroque Museum.** Artwork from the 17th and 18th century is presented. Especially noteable are the oil sketches and designs for altar paintings and murals *(☞ page 108).*

Through the arboured walk on the left side you'll reach the **Hedge Theatre,** which was modelled in 1717 after a French design and is the oldest of its kind in the German speaking world. The tall hedges

create a tiered theatrical backdrop with an orchestra pit in front. Behind it is the beginning of the

Bastion- or Dwarfs' Garden with its stone warf figures that depict different characters or professions.

In the small parterre in front of the castle you'll find the Pegasus Fountain, the winged horse made of hammered copper was made by sculptor Kaspar Glas in 1661.

The existing Mirabell castle no longer has the form of the Summer Residence or that of Altenau castle. At the beginning of the 18th century it was first rebuilt, then it was almost completely destroyed in the city fire of 1818. Only the *Marble Hall* on the first floor and the splendid stairway in the west wing with figures from Raphael Donner remained intact.

Today the office of the mayor and numerous other city offices are located in Mirabell castle. The Marble Hall is selected today by bridal couples from all over the world as a stylish ambience for their wedding ceremonies. Countless wedding photos have bee taken here with the impudent angels on the marble stairway or in front of Mirabell Gardens' many fountains.

In front of the castle extends the Mirabellplatz. Around the **Andräkirche** *(St.Andrew's Church)* you'll find a large open market every Thursday morning *(☞ page 96)*.

If you leave the park by way of the stairs flanked by two unicorns and

behind the Pegasus Fountain you'll come to the small spa park. The neighbouring *Spa House* has a swimming pool *(☞ page 100)* and is located near the *Conference Center.*

59

(35) Follow Rainerstraße to the left, away from the city about 400 m. and you'll reach the ***main train*** station. (☞ *You can, of course, reach the station with the bus, just two stops away.*) We will however turn right, cross Mirabellplatz, and head towards the city.

(36) We turn left down the Paris-Lodron-Straße where after 200 m. one finds on the right the inconspicuous building of the *Loreto Cloister.* The church and cloister were founded by Archbishop Paris Lodron at the beginning of the 17th century. It was destroyed during the big city fire and also during World War II and each time rebuilt in a simpler form. The visitors to the cloister's small pilgrimage church come mostly for the miraculous *"Loreto-Child"*, a little 11 cm. statue of the Christ

Child, splendidly attired and carved out of ivory.

(37) Right through the Bruderhof you'll reach the late Gothic **St.Sebastian's Church,** (1749-53), whose altars and paintings were also largely destroyed in the city fire. Noteworthy is the **St.Sebastian's Cemetery.** It was built

under Wolf Dietrich following an Italian model. In the square, surrounded by an arcade, you'll find the resting-place of many famous personalities, such as the doctor Paracelsus, Mozart's father, Leopold as well as Mozart's wife, Constanze. In the middle of the cemetery is the *Gabriel Chapel*, which is the mausoleum of Archbishop Wolf Dietrich von Raitenau.

Take a stroll through the *Linzergasse,* this is the shopping street on the right side of the Old Town, again in the direction of the river Salzach.

61

The short climb (about 5 min.) up the **Kapuzinerberg** *(Capuchin Mountain)* is also worthwhile (☞ through the archway by house Nr. 14, along the Stations of the Cross). From the **Hettwerbastei** *(Hettwer Bastion)* you have a beautiful view of the fortress and the Old Town. The **Kapuzinerkloster** *(Capuchin Monastery)* was founded in 1599 over the bastion and in keeping with monastic modesty and simplicity. Monks are still in residence

there today. The villa across from the monastery was the residence of poet and author **Stefan Zweig** from 1919-34.

When you have time you should definitely take a walk over the Kapuzinerberg. (☞ *Take Stefan-Zweig-Weg, it starts under the Capuchin Monastery.*

The way leads through the woods with its tall beech trees and offers delightful rest stops with marvellous views of the Old City on one side and the city district Schallmoos on the other. After about 20 minutes you'll reach the *Franziskischlössl,* which

was built by Archbishop Paris Lodron as a part of the city fortifications. Today it houses a small inn.

The *Imberg Steps* leads us again farther down from the Capuchin Monastery to the *Steingasse,* the oldest street in Salzburg. The residents of Steingasse were in earlier days the successful craftsmen of Salzburg and their representative houses with decorative arcaded walkways are today a favourite motiv for photos.

Salzburg in Winter

Salzburg also has a special flair in the winter months. During walks over the snow-covered city mountains you'll discover many wonderful views for photos. Church towers and the fortress show themselves capped in white and the gardens of Mirabell Castle disappear under a white carpet. In the time prior to Christmas the festively decorated shopping streets tempt you to shop and stroll.

Don't miss a visit to the **Christkindlmarkt** *(Christmas Market)* on the Domplatz and the **Advent-Singing** in the Festival Theatre.

Contemplative hours can be experienced in the pre-Christmas season by attending one of the many church concerts, hearing the **Salzburger Turmblasen** *(Salzburg Tower Brass)* or an excursion to the „**Stille**

Silent Night Chapel in Oberndorf

Nacht Kapelle" *(Silent Night Chapel)* in Oberndorf near Salzburg.

As the year draws to a close the Old Town takes on a festive turbulence. On New Year's Eve the sky is lit with a thousand colourful rockets as the evening is celebrated with dancing in all the streets, squares and bridges of the Old Town.

For the sportive, active guest, Salzburg is also a worthwhile winter destination. Its central location allows you to reach in less than an hour well-known ski areas such as *Sportwelt Ski Amadé, Obertauern, Zell am See or Kaprun*. All are equipped with state of the art chair and gondola-lifts, with hundreds of kilometres of the best prepared slopes and cross-country ski runs.

Salzburg's Surroundings

Leopoldskron Castle

(☞ The castle is a 20-minute walk from Nonntal, a part of the city south of the fortress.) The Rococo castle was built in 1736 by Archbishop v. Firmian for his family. From 1918-1956 it was owned by the Festival founder Max Reinhardt and later his heirs. It was a favourite meeting place for the prominent people of the Festival. Today, the castle is owned by an American Foundation and not opened to the public. The large adjacent pond attracts fishing fans and strollers alike. In winter, it beckons the ice-skaters.

The Stiegl World of Brewing

Fans of beer will find a lot of interesting things at the Stiegl World of Brewing, Europe's largest beer world of experience.

On a journey of discovery

The Stiegl World of Brewing conveys to beer aficionados any amount of essential information, instructive and strange alike, about beer: the hands-on-brewery lets you watch the master brewer at work making the beer of the month and, with a bit of luck, sample the freshly tapped beer. The "World of Beer" houses the largest beer tower in the world and beer fans can find out interesting facts about the drinking habits of the major beer-drinking nations. The beer museum exhibits original tools from long-forgotten eras. By the way, the admission fee includes tasting of the Stiegl beer specialities.

Dining at the brewery

A chilled pint goes down particularly well in the inviting Bräustüberl, the cosy Paracelsusstube or the shady beer garden. In the unique ambience surrounded by chestnut trees, a beer fountain and a view of the "old" mash house, beer fans can enjoy their freshly drawn tankard of Stiegl and fortify themselves with a Stiegl snack.

☞ *Museum: daily 10 am - 5 pm, July, August: 10 am - 7 pm (final admission one hour before closing) Gastronomy: daily 10 am - 12 pm Bus no. 1, station Bräuhausstraße* **www.brauwelt.at**

69

Anif Castle

The delightful castle surrounded by water is out of the 16th century and served as the summer residence of the archbishops of Chiemsee till 1814. Today the castle is privately owned and unfortunately not open to the public.

Hellbrunn

The *Pleasure castle Hellbrunn,* south of the city, was built in 1613-1619 under Archbishop Markus Sittikus following plans of Santino Solari the Cathedral's master builder. The castle with its state rooms and ballrooms, the free-standing double wing staircase and the splendid parks was not only meant for the relaxation and delight of the church - prince's illustrious guests. It was meant to mirror the power of the Salzburg Archbishops.

Unfortunately, little remains of the splendid furnishings. Worth seeing therefore is the masterfully glazed tile oven (1608) in the dining room as well as the illusionist, architectural vistas painted by Donato Mascagni, in the majestic hall which give the visitor the impression of wandering in a columned hall and in the *Oktogon* (the former music room), where the actual boundaries of the room are offset through painted corridors.

The large pleasure garden with its lovingly designed ponds and the old trees next to the castle is open to the public and is a very popular place for walks. You will also find the original **"Sound of Music pavilion"** here.

The **Steintheater** *(Stone Theatre)* in the east of the park is regarded as the oldest natural stage in the German speaking area. The first Italian opera performance north of the Alps was held here in 1617.

On Hellbrunn Mouintain stands the *"Monatsschlössl"* (about 1615), that Archbishop Markus Sittikus had built in supposedly the record time of one month as a guest-house. Today it houses the **Folklore Museum**. (☞ *page 108*)

The *"Wasserspiele"* (*Hellbrunn Trick Fountains*) are worth seeing (☞ *page 108*), where visitors are lead to grottoes, caves and arbours and can expect some rather wet surprises.

Table of the Archbishop, with trick fountains

Remarkable is the water driven *„Mechanical Theatre"* (1747-1752) with organ works and 256 figures depicting life in a small Baroque city.

Behind the large park, at the foot of the Hellbrunn Mountain you'll find the **Hellbrunn Zoo.** The large open enclosures and the many varieties of animals delight young and old alike. (☞ *page 108)*

From the **Untersberg** (1.853 m.) you'll have a marvellous view of Salzburg and its surroundings. It's easy to reach with the cable railway from St.Leonhard. (☞ *Use the autobahn exit* *Salzburg Süd. The railway operates daily from 8.30am - 5pm, in winter from 9am - 4pm).* Walks and hikes are popular over the Untersberg-Plateau to the *Salzburger Hochthron (ca. 30 min.)* or to the *Berchtesgadener Hochthron (ca. 2.30 hr.),* also the climb up to the **Schellenberger Eishöhle**, *(the largest ice cave in Germany, guided tours from the middle of May - middle of October, 9am - 5pm),* or the *Dopplersteig* to Glanegg. In the winter you can comfortably ski into the valley.

Salt mines and the Celtic Museum

15 kilometres south of Salzburg in Hallein you'll find the **Celtic Museum.** Tools and utensils out of the prehistoric salt mining age are shown and the finds from Celtic graves and settlements are displayed. In **Bad Dürrnberg,** above Hallein, where about 4.500 years ago salt was mined, one can view a reconstructed *Celtic settlement* and in the **salt-mine,** part of a tunnel

system is shown. A trip in a mining train, the salt sea, and a quick trip down one of the two long slides are the attractions of the tour.

(☞ *Open all year, April - Oct.: 9am - 5pm, November - March: 11am - 3pm*).

Salzburg Open Air Museum

Ten kilometres south west of Salzburg, near the village of Großgmain, is a 50 hectares park where farmhouses from the 16th -19th centuries are shown. These farmhouses represent all parts of the province of Salzburg.

They are for the most part furnished with original household items and tools. The farms are partly working farms and you

can observe local crafts-
men and artisans at work.

*(☞ open from Easter to the
end of October, Tuesday -
Sunday: 9am - 6pm).*

Klessheim Castle

The Baroque castle was built during 1700-1709 under
Archbishop Johann Thun from plans by Fischer von Erlach,
but it wasn't until after several changes and reconstruction
that Archbishop Leopold Firmian occupied the building in
1732. The stag with stars on its antlers is his heraldic animal
and stands in front of the castle. Since 1921, it has been under
provincial ownership and today with its stylish ambience is
used for the Salzburg Casino.

Maria Plain

The pilgrimage church, Maria Plain, is visible for miles around. Located on the northern edge of the city, it was built in 1671 - 1674. Stations of the Cross, line the way up to the church on the Kalvarienberg. The richly appointed

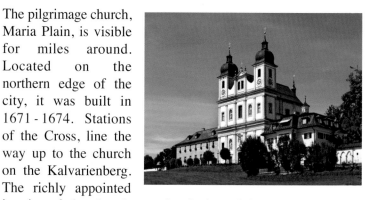

interior of the church remains in its original Baroque style. Displayed in the middle of the high altar is a painting of the Virgin Mary, surrounded by a golden halo. It originates from the Bavarian area and there in 1633 remained miraculously unscathed after a large fire. It is thus seen as having miraculous powers. One should also notice the elaborate wrought-iron grill work (1683) in front of the high altar.

Gaisberg

Situated in the east of Salzburg, the *Gaisberg* (1.288 m) with a transmitting station on its summit plateau is easy to recognize. It also offers beautiful views of Salzburg and to the foothills of the Alps. Hiking *(circular hiking path starts at Gastof Zistel)* and paragliding *(starting at the summit plateau)* are popular when there is beautiful weather.

Excursions in the Province of Salzburg

Werfen

45 km. south of Salzburg, locked in the Salzach Valley is the **Hohenwerfen Castle,** situated on a steep hill at the narrow pass between the Tennengebirge and the Hagengebirge. It was built in 1077 and is thus the same age as the Hohensalzburg Fortress (*☞ open from the beginning of April to the beginning of November*).

Today besides the guided tour of the castle one can see a large weapon exhibition and a falconry museum. One can also experience the ***Bird of Prey Show*** by the *Salzburg Landesfalkenhof.*

In the rock wall across from the castle, at a height of 1.600 meters, one finds the entrance to ***"Eisriesenwelt",*** the largest ice cave in the world.

(42 m. long) A guide directs you to a fascinating realm of eternal ice, shows you colossal columns, giant vaults and bizarre formations and lets the ice shine with splendid colours (*☞ guided tours from May to the beginning of October*).

Großglockner

The **Großglockner Hochalpenstraße,** built between 1930-35, is one of the most beautiful mountain passes in Europe. *(A toll road open to traffic from the beginning of May to*

October, depending on snow.) The drive from Salzachtal to Heiligenblut offers landscape and views that are unforgettable. The road leads up through the *"Ravine of the Bears"*, through romantic alpine pastures, and through the wildly carved rock formations of *"Witches' Kitchen"* to the **Fuscher Törl.**

The road branches off to **Edelweißspitze** (2.571 metres), which is the highest point of the Glocknerstraße. Here you'll find a breathtaking view. On clear days you can see 37 mountain all over 3.000 metres high, 19 mountain glaciers and hundred of other peaks.

The road leads further over the *Fuscher Törl,* through the *Hochtor* and again down in the direction of Heiligenblut. At the halfway point the road divides to **Kaiser-Franz-Josefs-Höhe** where you will have the

Großglockner (3.798m.) right before your eyes. With an inclined railway you come down to the *Pasterzengletscher*, the largest glacier of the eastern Alps, measuring 10 km. long.

Along the road you will find "Information-Stops" where you can learn more about the animal, plant and mountain life of this high mountain region.

(☞ *Don't miss a visit to the large deer- and game park next to the toll station in Fernleiten).*

Kaiser Franz-Josefs-Höhe

The Salzkammergut

An excursion to the nearby **Salzkammergut** *(Salzburg Lake District)* offers you a wealth of unforgettable impressions. In summer, one can swim in the beautiful clear lakes embedded between the mountains. The numerous peaks beckon you to hike and offer a glorious panoramic view to be enjoyed. Of course, there are also the well-known holiday locations, *Mondsee, St.Gilgen and St.Wolfgang*, with its famous *"Weisses Rössl"*, and the old *"City of the Emperor"*, Bad Ischl.

From Salzburg one drives along the Salzkammergut Bundesstraße 158 through the rolling foothills of the Alps to the east. Soon after the village of Hof (18 km) look to the left to **Fuschlsee** *(Lake Fuschl)*, 4 km long and very clear. On a small promontory is **Fuschl**

Castle. Formerly the hunting lodge of the prince-archbishops, it is today a stylish restaurant. Five kilometres farther you reach a small lakeside resort area.

Fuschl am See.

Here you will find all kinds of possibilities for water sports. The idyllic hiking trail around the lake is definitely worth recommending, *(ca. 9 km)* as is an excursion to the *Wartenfels Ruin* on the lower half of the Schober Mountain.

Over a hill you'll reach **Wolfgangsee** *(Lake Wolfgang - 11 km long, 114 m deep)* encircled by high mountains and probably the most romantic lake of the Salzkammergut.

St.Gilgen
am Wolfgangsee

This small spot with its beautiful lake promenade is one of the most popular holiday and lakeside resorts in the area. Don't overlook the frescoes and the façade of the Post Hotel and the frescoes in the cemetery chapel (18th century). A cable railway leads up to the Zwölferhorn, from where you can enjoy a marvellous view of the whole lake and numerous mountaintops.

The mountain is a popular ski area in winter.

St.Gilgen is also well known as the birthplace of *Anna Pertl*, the daughter of an archiepiscopal administrator. She was later married to the musician Leopold Mozart and was the mother of *Wolfgang Amadeus Mozart*. In the house where she was born, is a museum commemorating the life and time of Mozart. Mozart's sister Nannerl lived here for 17 years after she became the wife of the administrator, Berchthold.

Don't miss the hiking trail along the lake to the picturesque *Fürbergbucht (Fürberg Cove)* and further up the *Falkensteinwand* with a hermitage and a little pilgrimage church honouring St.Wolfgang. From the summit of the perpendicular dropping face of the

Mozart Fountain

Falkensteinwand (150 m high) the boats below on the lake appear to be toys at your feet.

(☞ *Follow the path down to Ried and rent a boat for the trip back to St.Gilgen)*

83

Also rewarding is an excursion over to **Lake Mondsee** (11 km long). Along the street you can find many beautiful swimming spots. A few kilometres farther you'll reach the village.

Mondsee,

the little town was already settled during the Stone Age and flourished during the time of the Romans. The Bavarian Duke Odilio II founded in 748 the local monastery on Roman ruins. This foundation influenced the culture of the Mondsee region for more than 1000 years.

The village centre is characterised by the late Gothic collegiate church (1470-1487), the second oldest church in Upper Austria. The splendid Baroque interior is surrounded with among other things 13 altars. Worth pointing out is the **Corpus-Christi-Altar** from artist Meinrad

Guggenbichler with the famous „Kindln" cherubs carrying grapes.

Don't miss a trip to the **Rauchhaus,** *(Smoke House)* an old fashioned styled farm with an open stove.

From St.Gilgen we drive along the Salzkammergut Bundesstrasse around Wolfgangsee and take a side trip to

St.Wolfgang,

St.Wolfgang is the village that got its worldwide reputation through an operetta. Two comedy producers from Berlin, during a visit in the Salzkammergut, were inspired to create a comical tale, setting it in St.Wolfgang because of its beauty. In 1929 Ralph Benatzky composed music to accompany it, Robert Stolz and others contributed hits and a world success was born. And so today, thousands of tourists come annually to see the famous *"Weisse Rössl on Wolfgangsee"*.

Particularly during the summer months there is always a hubbub in the narrow streets in the centre of the village. Don't let this drive you away and notice the many little details, lovingly made, on some of the very old houses.

Standing directly on the banks of the lake is the *Church of St.Wolfgang*. During the Middle Ages it was the most visited pilgrimage church in the entire German Speaking region. The reason was the popularity of Saint Wolfgang, who in 976 withdrew to a hermitage on Falkenstein between St.Wolfgang and St.Gilgen and the legend, says built a chapel on this spot.

The splendid interior of today's church characterised by the marvellous winged altar by Michael Pacher (1481), a marvel in the art of woodcarving. The gilded middle group is a crowned Mary in front of the divine son, framed by 16 large and 4 small elaborate panels.

The **Schafberg** (1783) is St.Wolfgang's third largest attraction. You can reach the summit on foot or with the rack railway established in 1893. The trip with the romantic old steam locomotive or the modern diesel-railcar takes about one hour and is a special experience for young and old. (☞ *Service from the beginning of May through the middle of October*)

The panorama from the summit of the Schafberg is of incomparable beauty. The north side of the mountain drops with an almost perpendicular rock wall. One stands as if on a pulpit with Mondsee below, with views of Attersee and the foothills of the Alps reaching to the Danube. The view from the south side overlooks the full length of Wolfgangsee, and on a clear day one can see over 100 mountaintops. (☞ *Sit in the inn on the sunny terrace in the peace of the colossal panorama.*)

Another lovely experience is a trip on one of the regularly scheduled boat trips across Wolfgangsee. Especially popular is the 110-year-old paddle steamer *„Franz Josef I"*. The ships have mooring spots in every village so you can get off,

enjoy a stroll and later continue your trip. *(☞ According to the service timetable from the beginning of May to the middle of October).*

After driving 13 kilometres from the end of Wolfgangsee you'll reach

Bad Ischl.

This little spot became famous as the summer holiday of the Austrian *Emperor Franz Joseph* and as the health resort for the prominent of the Austrian-Hungarian monarchy. It was here in 1853 that the Emperor celebrated his engagement to his future bride, the *Princess Elizabeth (Sisi)* from Bavaria. His summer residence, the *Kaiservilla,* is more simply furnished and is more impressive by its surrounding nature than through structural sophistication. One can't miss the thousands of hunting trophies - Emperor Franz Joseph was an enthusiastic hunter!

The romantic little **marble castle** in the park of the Kaiservilla was the favourite abode of Empress Sisi and serves today as a photo-museum and the backdrop for openings and presentations.

Also worth seeing are the feudal spa rooms and beautiful spa gardens, the **Lehar Museum** and the charming shopping streets.

(☞ *Don't forget to stroll down the the promenade along the Traun River and visit the famous and elegant Konditorei Zauner to experience a typical Austrian sweet or dessert.*)

Hallstatt

The picturesque salt-mining village, 22 km from Bad Ischl, was built into the steep slope that drops off to the Hallstätter See.

A settlement already existed here in 2.500 BC. It has therefore become famous for its extensive grave finds from the epoch 800-400 BC, the „Hallstatt Time". Old houses, narrow streets, full of corners, a triangular market place, and two striking churches colour the picture of the village.

The late Gothic church with its Baroque tower was built into carved out rock high up. It holds many beautiful frescoes, an elaborate carved and gilded high altar from Leonhard Astl (1520), and also a smaller winged altar from 1420.

Next to the church is the famous *"Beinhaus"* of Hallstatt, where over 1.200 skulls and bones lie piled up. Space was scarce in the cemetery and so the dead were soon taken from their graves and laid here to rest.

Those who wish to visit the *„Oldest salt mine in the world"* must take the funicular railway into Hochtal. Here you'll also find the famous burial ground and archeological finds of the Hallstatt Zeit. A brine pipe was used as early as 1595 to transport the dissolved salt to the drying area, a distance of 40 kilometres. This was certainly a masterpiece for those early times.

If you visit Hallstatt on the feast of Corpus Christi, you can witness the famous **procession.** The holy monstrance is taken on a boat decorated with flowers across the lake accompanied by many other decorated boats and barges.

On the opposite side of the lake from Hallstatt, in **Obertraun,** one can climb to the famous Dachstein Caves. The **Mammuthöhle**

extends in several stories over a cave of 300 metres, in the **Dachsteineishöhle** you can admire the sophisticated lighting of the ice dome and in the **Koppenbrüllerhöhle** be enchanted by the limestone patterns and shapes.

Gosausee

A hiking trail along the front Gosausee and further to the back Gosausee offers diverse impressions of the marvellous natural environment. The deep blue lake is situated peacefully between rocky and partly steep slopping embankments, the jagged peaks of the abrupt Gosaukammes (ridge) and the snow covered Dachstein Mountains reflected in the calm crystal clear water. A cable railway leads from the front Gosausee up the Zwieselalm, from where the view of the lakes and the powerful Dachstein is even more fascinating.

INFORMATIONS

Information Offices

Mozartplatz Information Office, Mozartplatz 5	Tel. 88987-330
Main-Train-Station, passage	Tel. 88987-340
Salzburg-Süd, Park & Ride area Alpenstrasse	Tel. 88987-360
Wals-Himmelreich, Walser Bundesstrasse 23	Tel. 851067

Tourism Salzburg GmbH - Salzburg Information
(management, marketing, administration)
5020 Salzburg, Auerspergstr. 6   Tel. 88987-0

Salzburg State Board of Tourism
5300 Hallwang, Wiener Bundesstr. 23   Tel. 6688

Important Telephon Numbers

Fire Department	Tel. 122
Police	Tel. 133
Rescue	Tel. 144

Telephone Information   Tel. 11811 or Tel. 118899

Taxi   Tel. 1715 or Tel. 2220 or Tel. 8111

Automobile Breakdown: ÖAMTC   Tel. 120
                       ARBÖ   Tel. 123

Train Information   Tel. 051717
Flight Information, Salzburg Aiport Services   Tel. 8580-251

Medical Assistance

Accident Hospital, Dr.Franz-Rehrl-Platz 5   Tel. 6580-0
Provincial Hospital, Müllner Hauptstr. 48   Tel. 4482-0
Provincial Psychiatric Clinic, Ignaz-Harrer-Str. 79   Tel. 4483-0
Diakonissen Krankenhaus, Guggenbichlerstr. 20   Tel. 6385-0
Barmherzige Brüder, Kajetanerplatz 1   Tel. 8088-0

Emergency Medical Service, Dr.Karl-Renner-Str. 7   Tel. 141
        Only Friday 7pm - Monday 7am and holidays
Dental Emergency Service (Sat. Sun. and holidays)   Tel. 870022

Pharmacies - Night and Weekend Service
The respective emergency services can be found listed in the daily
newspaper or posted at every pharmacy.

Opening Times

Post Offices: Mon - Thu: 8am - 12, 2pm - 6pm;
Fri: 8am - 12, 2pm - 5pm;

Banks: Mon. - Fri: 8.30am - 12.30, 2pm - 4.30pm
Salzburg has a network of automatic teller machines
(ATM) where one can get service around the clock.

Pharmacies: Mon - Fri: 8am - 12.30, 2.30pm - 6pm,
Sat: 8am - 12;
Emergency service available nights and weekends

Farmers' Markets:
Grünmarkt, Universitätsplatz: Mon - Fri: 6am-6pm, Sat: 6am-1pm;
Schrannenmarkt, Mirabellplatz: Thu: 6am - 1pm (except holidays)

Fortress Railway: Festungsgasse 4; May - August: 9am - 10pm,
September: 9am - 9pm, October - April: 9am - 5pm

Public Transportation

at all Information Locations as well as Public Transit Authority,
Informationsbüro der Verkehrsbetriebe, Schrannengasse 4 (Mirabell-
platz). Tickets are available on all means of Public transportation.
Reduced price tickets are available in every Trafik (Tobacconist's
Shop), the Information Office of the Transit Authority, as well as at
numerous bus stops.

Eating and Drinking

In Salzburg You'll find every category of restaurant and inn, from top
gourmet restaurants to fast food spots. Typical Austrian specialities
are served above all (☞ *page 106*). The brochure "Eating and Drinking
in Salzburg" gives a complete overview of dining establishments in
Salzburg and is free at all Information Offices. Also included is an
overview of the beer pubs, wine bars, cafes and nightclubs.

Accommodations

In all Salzburg City Information Offices is a list of all hotels, inns and private rooms for rent.

Youth Hostels
Jugendgästehaus Salzburg, Josef-Preis-Allee 18   tel. 842984-0
Jugendherberge Aigen, Aigner Str. 34   tel. 623248
Eduard-Heinrich-Haus, Eduard-Heinrich-Str. 2   tel. 625976

Campgrounds
Panorama Camping-Rauchenbichl, Salzburg-Nord,
    Rauchenbichlerstr. 21   tel. 450652
Camping Nord-Sam, Salzburg-Nord, Samstr. 22a   tel. 660494

Salzburger Festungskonzerte

Events

End of January	Mozart Week
Easter Week	Easter Festival
Whitsun (Pfingsten)	Town Fair (Dult)
End of July to end of August	Salzburg Festival
Beginning of August	Festival in Hellbrunn
24. September	Town Fair (Rupertikirtag)
End of November - 23. Dez.	Christmas-Market on Cathedral Square, at Hellbrunn and various other Christmas Markets
	Advent Singing

Music, Theatre

Salzburger Landestheater, Schwarzstr. 22	tel. 871512
Elisabethbühne, Petersbrunnhof, Erzabt-Klotz-Str. 22	tel. 8085-0
Kleines Theater, Schallmooser Hauptstr. 50	tel. 872154-0
Marionettentheater, Schwarzstr. 24	tel. 872406
Festungskonzerte, Anton Adelgasser Weg 22	tel. 825858
Mozart Serenaden, Lieferinger Hauptstr. 136	tel. 436870
Rockhouse, Schallmooser Hauptstr. 46	tel. 884914
Toi-Haus, Franz-Josef-Str. 4	tel. 874439

Cinemas

Elmo-Kino-Center, St.Julienstr. 5	tel. 872373
Das Kino, Gisela-Kai 11	tel. 873100
Cineplexx, Airportcenter	tel. 850101
Cineplexx, Salzburg City, Main Train Station	tel. 460101

IMPORTANT ADDRESSES

Car Rental

Available at the Salzburg Airport, the Main Train Station as well as in the following offices:

Arac, Vogelweiderstr. 69	tel. 871616
AVIS, Ferd.-Porsche-Str. 7	tel. 877278
Buchbinder, Vogelweiderstr. 63	tel. 882066
Budget, Innsbrucker Bundesstr. 95	tel. 855038
Denzel Drive, Gabelsbergerstr. 3	tel. 050105-4160
Hertz, Ferd.-Porsche-Str. 7	tel. 876674

Swimming Pools

Paracelsus Hallenbad, (indoor pool) Auerspergstr. 2	tel. 883544
Freibad Alpenstraße	tel. 620832
Freibad Leopoldskron, Leopoldskronstr. 50	tel. 829265
Freibad Volksgarten, Hermann-Bahr-Promenade 2	tel. 623183

Libraries

Stadtbibliothek, Schuhmacherstr. 14	tel. 8072-2450
Universitätsbibliothek, Hofstallgasse 2-4	tel. 8044 -77550

Ice Skating

Eis-Arena, H. Bahr-Promenade 2   tel. 623411-0
      (middle of September - end of March)

Bike Rental

a'VELO, Willibald-Hauthaler-Str. 10   tel. 435595
      Eastern - beginning of October also Residenzplatz
Biker's Best, Fürstenallee 39   tel. 823723
Top Bike Salzburg, Hauptbahnhof und Staatsbrücke
                              tel. 0676 4767259

Guide Service
Salzburg Guide Service, Getreidegasse 31   tel. 840406

Lost and Found
Mirabell Castle   tel. 8072-0
Main Train Station   tel. 93000-22222

Guest Kindergardens
Privatkindergarten Eder, Göllstr. 3   tel. 829196
Privatkindergarten Haunspergstr. 23   tel. 877262

Luggage Storage
Main Train Station, 0-24 Uhr   tel. 93000-3186

Ticket Officies:
Salzburg Ticket Service, Mozartplatz 5   tel. 840310
Kartenzentrale Polzer, Residenzplatz 3   tel. 8969
Raiffeisen Ticketservice, Schwarzstr. 9   tel. 8886-1722
Ticket Shop, Getreidegasse 5   tel. 847767
Salzburger Festspiele, H.v.Karajan-Platz 11   tel. 8045 500

Sightseeing Flights
Airlink-Salzburg Airport,
    Innsbrucker Bundesstr. 95   tel. 850863-0

Post Offices
Main Train Station: Monday - Friday 6.30am - 9.30pm.
    Saturday 8am - 8pm.
    Sunday 1pm - 6pm.   Tel. 450550-0
Post-offices in the inner city: Residenzplatz, Makartplatz,
    Schrannengasse, Neutorstraße, Nonntaler Hauptstraße
    Mon - Thu: 8am - 12am, 2pm. - 6pm;
    Fri: 8am - 12am, 2pm - 5pm.;

Police Stations

Main Train Station	tel. 059133 - 55 - 82100
Rathaus (Altstadt), Rudolfskai 2	tel. 059133 - 55 - 88100
Maxglan, Maxglaner Hauptstr. 72	tel. 059133 - 55 - 87100
Gnigl, Minnesheimstr. 20	tel. 059133 - 55 - 84100
Itzling, Jakob-Haringer-Str. 5a	tel. 059133 - 55 - 85100
Lehen, Rudolf-Biebl-Str. 41	tel. 059133 - 55 - 86100
Taxham, Europark, Europastr. 1	tel. 059133 - 55 - 89100
Polizeidirektion, Alpenstr. 88	tel. 059133 - 55 - 81100

Casino

Located in Klessheim castle, Autobahn exit Klessheim, opens daily at 3pm, free Casino-Shuttle-Bus at Mirabellplatz and the Mönchsberg Lift from 2:30pm hourly.

City Tours

Salzburg Panorama Tours, Mirabellplatz   tel. 874029

Salzburg Sightseeing Tours, Mirabellplatz   tel. 881616

Fiaker, Residenzplatz   tel. 435894

Taxi

You'll find these taxi stands in the city: Hanuschplatz, Residenzplatz, Makartplatz, Rudolfsplatz, central-station, Mönchsberg-lift, Franz-Josef-Straße, Unfallkrankenhaus

tel. 1715   or   tel. 2220   or   tel. 8111

ORIGINAL

MOZARTHAUS
SALZBURG

MOZARTHAUS - A COMPANY OF THE
INTERNATIONAL MOZART FOUNDATION

SHOPS

MOZART'S BIRTHPLACE • GETREIDEGASSE 9
OPEN DAILY FROM 9AM -6 PM

MOZART'S RESIDENCE • MAKARTPLATZ 8
OPEN DAILY FROM 9AM - 6PM

INTERNATIONAL MAIL-ORDERING

MOZARTHAUS HANDELS- UND VERSANDGESELLSCHAFT
OF INTERNATIONAL MOZART FOUNDATION GES.M.B.H.

A-5020 SALZBURG • MAKARTPLATZ 8
www.mozarthaus.biz   e-mail: office@mozarthaus.biz   Fax: +43 662 872924

Wolfgange Amadeo Mozart

TIPS

Parking

The entire city centre has short term pay-parking zones. (3hr. limit)
Parking permits are available from ticket machines on the side-
walks. During high season parking places in the city centre are
filled. It is recommended to park outside of the inner city and use
public transportation to reach destinations in the centre.

Park&Ride Parkplatz Süd, Alpenstraße
Park&Ride Parkplatz Mitte, Salzburger Ausstellungszentrum
(only during July and August, as pay-parking)

Dining

A worthwhile address in the city centre:

Stiftskeller St. Peter – Pleasure and Tradition
Salzburg hospitality since 1803. Charm and history in every corner
of the house. Exceptional ambiance and traditional cuisine turn
a visit into an experience. Food service is available throughout
the day. The Mozart Dinner-Concerts are held in Salzburg's most
beautiful Baroque hall.

In the Salzburg surroundings:

Grünauerhof, Wals, Autobahn exit Salzburg-Wals (West): spacious, large portions.

Shopping

Europark Shopping Centre, Autobahn exit Klessheim: 130 shops and restaurants under one roof! 4.200 free parking spaces.
Open: Mon. - Fri.: 9am - 7:30pm / Saturday: 9am - 5pm

Mozart Residence: CD-shop specialized in Mozart-CD's and Mozart-souvenirs

Mozart's Birthplace: exquisite Mozart-souvenirs

Something Special for the Kids!

House of Nature (Feeding the sharks - every monday at 10:30 am; Feeding the crocodiles: Wed. 4pm, (only in the summer months)

Hellbrunn Zoo: In every season, in any weather!
A free flying griffon; a petting zoo for the little visitors; in the summer, every friday and saturday the "zoo at night".

Wasserspiel Hellbrunn - Trick Fountains of Hellbrunn: Fun for both young and old!

Evenings
The Salzburg night life is centered at locations on both sides of the river Salzach from the Staatsbrücke (bridge) in the direction leading upriver.

MUSEUM OPENING-HOURS

Catacombs: St.Peter's cemetery; May - Sept.: 10.30 am - 5 pm
Oct. - April: Wed. and Thurs.: 10.30 am - 3.30 pm, Fri. - Sun.: 10.30 am - 4 pm
(conducted tours only)

Cathedral Museum: Entrance of the Cathedral; Cathedral treasure, curiosity
chamber from the 17th and 18th centuries. May - October, December: Mon.- Sat.:
10 am - 5 pm, Sun. and public holiday: 11 am - 6 pm

Cathedral Excavations: Residenzplatz; Excavations of the medieval cathedral and
roman remains; July and August: daily 9 am - 5 pm

Festival Halls: Hofstallgasse; July, August: 9.30 am, 2 pm, 3.30 pm;
June, Septenber: 2 pm, 3.30 pm, October - May: 2 pm; (conducted tours only)

Folklore Museum: Hellbrunn, Monatsschlössl; Folk art and customs, devotional objects;
April - October: daily 10 am - 5.30 pm

Fortress Hohensalzburg: Central Europe's largest, completely preserved fortress
dating from the 11th century.
Fortress-Museum (fortress history, weapons) and **Marionette Museum:**
Oct. - April: 9.30 am - 5 pm; May - Sept.: 9 am - 7 pm

Fortress cable railway: Jan. - April: 9 am - 5 pm; May, June and Sept: 9 am - 8 pm;
July, Aug.: 9 am - 10 pm; Oct. - Dec.: 9 am - 5 pm

Haydn-Memorial: St.Peter's District; scores and private objects of Haydn;
May, June, Oct.: Thurs.- Tues.: 2 - 5 pm; July - Sept: Thurs.- Tues.: 12.30 - 5 pm

Museum of Natural History: Museumsplatz 5; Aquarium, reptile-zoo, space-
discoveryhall, sea-world; daily 9 am - 5 pm

Hellbrunn - Pleasure Castle, Trick Fountains (conducted tours only):
April, Oct. and Nov.: 9 am - 4.30 pm, May, June and Sept.: 9 am - 5.30 pm;
July, August: 9 am - 6 pm (also evening tours at 7 pm, 8 pm and 9 pm)

Hellbrunn Zoo: Open all year round from 9 am; August: also "Night-Zoo" -
every Friday and Saturday night until 11 pm, last entrance 9.30 pm

Mozart's Birthplace: Getreidegasse 9; Burgher's house; instruments, letters,
portraits of the Mozart family; daily from 9 am - 5.30 pm;
July, August: daily from 9 am - 8 pm

Mozart Residence: Makartplatz 8; history of the building, life of the Mozart family;
daily from 9 am - 5.30 pm; July, August: daily from 9 am - 8 pm

Mozart Sound and Film Collection: Mozart's Residence; archive contains material relating to the interpretation of Mozart's work, documentary and feature films; Mon, Tues. and Fri.: 9 am - 1 pm, Wed. and Thurs.: 1 pm - 5 pm

Museum of Modern Art Mönchsberg: Mönchsberg 32;
Museum of Modern Art Rupertinum: Wiener-Philharmoniker-Gasse 9;
20th and 21st century paintings, graphic art, sculpture and photography.
Tues. - Sun.: 10 am - 6 pm; Wed.: 10 am - 8 pm; (open Mon. during festival periods)

Panorama Museum New Residence: Residenzplatz 9, entrance through the post-office; Round painting with a historic view of the city;
daily from 9 am - 5 pm; Thurs.: 9 am - 8 pm

Residence Gallery: Residenzplatz 1; European paintings 16th - 19th century.;
Tues. - Sun.: 10 am - 5 pm; open Monday during Easter, festival and Christmas periods)

Residence State Rooms: Residenzplatz 1; Former official apartments of the Salzburg prince-archbishops; daily from 10 am - 5 pm

Salzburg Baroque Museum: Mirabell garden, Orangerie; the exhibits on display are firstrate examples of the creativeprocess behind the monumental works of the 17th and 18th centuries.
Wed. - Sun: 10 am - 5 pm; July, Aug: Tues. - Sun.: 10 am - 5 pm

Salzburg City Cruise Line: Makartsteg;
April: 1 pm - 4 pm; May, June: 11 am - 5 pm; July, August: 11 am - 7 pm;
Sept.: 12 - 5 pm; Oct.: 2 - 4 pm

Salzburg Museum: New Residence, Mozartplatz 1; Exiting insights into Salzburg's history, art and culture; Tues. - Sun.: 9 am - 5 pm, Thurs: 9 am - 8 pm;
in July, August and December also Monday: 9 am - 5 pm

Stiegl World of Brewing: Bräuhausstr. 9;
Europe's unique adventure brewery, beer-tasting; daily from 10 am - 5 pm;
July, August: 10 am - 7 pm; final entrance one hour before closing.
Gastronomy: daily 10 am - 12 pm

Toy Museum: Bürgerspitalgasse 2; Toy-collection and historical musical instruments;
Tues. - Sun.: 9 am- 5 pm; in July, Aug. and Dec. also Mon.: 9 am - 5 pm

Trakl-Memorial and Research Centre: Waagplatz 1a; Material pertaining to the poet's life; Mon. - Fri.: 11 am and 2 pm (conducted tours only)

The opening hours listed are correct for most of the year. Changes and variations may occur during certain seasons.

INDEX

Map Information

Parkplatz
Parking Lots
Parcheggio
Parking
Aparcamiento
Парковка
パーキング
露天停車場

 Parkgarage
Parking garages
Garage coperto
Parking souterrain
Garage
Подземный гараж
屋内駐車場
室内停車場

 Park & Ride
Parcheggio interscambio
駐車場 ＆ バス停
公交轉運處

 Busterminal
Terminal d'autocars
Terminal dei bus
Terminal de Buses
Автобусный терминал
バス・ターミナル
大巴士停泊處

 Campingplatz
Camping
Campeggio
Campings
Кемпинг
キャンプ場
露営地

 Information
Informazioni
Información
Информация
インフォメーション
旅遊諮詢處

 Postamt
Post Offices
Ufficio postale
Bureau de poste
Correo
Почта
郵便局
郵局

 öffentliches WC
Public Toilets
WC pubblico
Toilettes publiques
Baños públicos
Туалеты
公衆トイレ
公共廁所

 Jugendherberge
Youth Hostels
Ostello per la gioventù
Auberge de jeunesse
Albergue juvenil
Молодежные турбазы
ユースホステル
青年旅社

 Aussichtspunkt
Spot commanding a
good view
Punta della vista bella
Point de vue
Смотровая площадка
展望台
瞭望台